SOP for Monitoring Black Oystercatchers — Version 1.1

Southwest Alaska Inventory and Monitoring Network

Natural Resource Report NPS/SWAN/NRR—2011/391

James L. Bodkin[1]

[1]U.S. Geological Survey
Alaska Science Center,
4210 University Dr
Anchorage, AK 99508

May 2011

U.S. Department of the Interior
National Park Service
Natural Resource Program Center
Fort Collins, Colorado

The National Park Service, Natural Resource Program Center publishes a range of reports that address natural resource topics of interest and applicability to a broad audience in the National Park Service and others in natural resource management, including scientists, conservation and environmental constituencies, and the public.

The Natural Resource Report Series is used to disseminate high-priority, current natural resource management information with managerial application. The series targets a general, diverse audience, and may contain NPS policy considerations or address sensitive issues of management applicability. All manuscripts in the series receive the appropriate level of peer review to ensure that the information is scientifically credible, technically accurate, appropriately written for the intended audience, and designed and published in a professional manner. This report received formal peer review by subject-matter experts who were not directly involved in the collection, analysis, or reporting of the data, and whose background and expertise put them on par technically and scientifically with the authors of the information.

Views, statements, findings, conclusions, recommendations, and data in this report are those of the author(s) and do not necessarily reflect views and policies of the National Park Service, U.S. Department of the Interior. Mention of trade names or commercial products does not constitute endorsement or recommendation for use by the National Park Service.

This report is available from the Southwest Alaska Inventory & Monitoring Network website (http://science.nature.nps.gov/im/units/swan/index.cfm?theme=brown_bear) and the Natural Resource Publications Management website (http://www.nature.nps.gov/publications/nrpm/).

Please cite this publication as:

Bodkin, J. L. 2011. SOP for monitoring black oystercatchers - Version 1.1: Southwest Alaska Inventory and Monitoring Network. Natural Resource Report NPS/SWAN/NRR—2011/391. National Park Service, Fort Collins, Colorado.

NPS 953/107685, May 2011

Revision History Log

All edits and amendments made to this document since its inception should be recorded in the table below. Users of this protocol should promptly notify the project leader of the marine nearshore monitoring program of recommended edits or changes. The project leader will review and incorporate suggested changes as necessary, record these changes in the revision history log, and modify the date and version number on the title page of this document to reflect these changes.

Revision History Log:

Previous Version #	Revision Date	Author	Changes Made	Reason for Change	New Version #
Version 1	10/6/09	Coletti	Formatting; updating to reflect SWAN	To meet NRR standards, remove NGEM references	1.1
Version 1.1	09/01/10	Coletti	Formatting; updating to reflect SWAN		NA
Version 1.1	03/08/2011	Bodkin	Final review		NA
Add rows as needed for each change or set of changes associated with each version.					

Contents

Contents (continued)

Figures

Tables

Appendices

1 Background and Objectives

1.1 Introduction
The purpose of this standard operating protocol (SOP) is to describe the justification, sampling design and process for collecting, recording, and analyzing data related to monitoring the nest density, nest occupancy, and diet of the black oystercatcher (*Haematopus bachmani*) under the SWAN nearshore monitoring program at Katmai (KATM) and Kenai Fjords (KEFJ) National Parks.

The black oystercatcher was selected for inclusion into the nearshore SWAN Inventory and Monitoring program because: 1) it is a common and conspicuous member of the rocky and gravel intertidal marine communities of eastern Pacific shorelines, 2) it is completely dependent on nearshore marine habitats for all critical life history components including foraging, breeding, chick-rearing, and resting (Andres and Falxa 1995), 3) it serves as a "keystone" species that is important in structuring nearshore systems, and 4) it is highly susceptible to human disturbance. During the spring/summer breeding season pairs establish and defend both nest and forage areas, and these territories and nest sites can persist over many years (Groves 1984, Hazlitt and Butler 2001) with individual life expectancy exceeding 15 years (Andres and Falxa 1995). Nest sites occur along a variety of shorelines, including consolidated and unconsolidated sediments, usually just slightly above the high-high tidal level (Vermeer et al. 1992, Andres 1998). The diet consists primarily of mussels (*Mytilus* sp) and a variety of limpets (*Lottia, Tectura, Acmea, and Colisella spp.*) (Andres and Falxa 1995), both ecologically and socially important constituents of the intertidal community. The species is considered a Management Indicator Species by the Chugach National Forest (Chugach National Forest 2003) and a species of concern by the Alaska Shorebird Working Group (Brown et al. 2001) and is widely recognized as a species representative of nearshore habitats and therefore particularly amenable to long term monitoring (Lentfer and Maier 1995, Andres 1998).

1.2 Rationale for Monitoring Black Oystercatchers
As a "keystone" species (Power et al. 1996), the black oystercatcher has a large influence on the structure of intertidal communities that is disproportionate to its abundance. The black oystercatcher receives its recognition as a keystone species through a three-trophic-level cascade initiated by the oystercatcher as a top level consumer in the nearshore (Marsh 1986, Hahn and Denny 1989, Falxa 1992) whose diet consists largely of gastropod (limpets) and bivalve (mussels) mollusks that are ecologically important in the intertidal community. As a consequence of oystercatcher foraging, large numbers of herbivorous limpets can be removed (Frank 1982, Lindberg et al. 1987), resulting in shifts in limpet species composition and size distribution (Marsh 1986, Lindberg et al. 1987). As a consequence of reduced limpet densities and the reduced grazing intensity that results, algal populations respond through increased production and survival, resulting in enhanced algal populations (Marsh 1986, Meese 1990, Wootton 1992, Lindberg et al. 1998). Additionally, the oystercatcher's diet consists of a large fraction of mussels, an important filter feeding bivalve that provides energy to a wide array of invertebrate, avian, and mammalian predators (Knox 2000, Menge and Branch 2001). Because the oystercatcher brings limpets and mussels back to its nest to provision chicks, collections of shell remains at nests provides an opportunity to obtain an independent sample of the species composition and size distribution of prey (Webster 1941, Frank 1982, Marsh 1986, Lindberg et

al. 1987). The collection of black oystercatcher diet and prey data offers a unique perspective into processes structuring nearshore communities (Marsh, 1986, Lindberg et al. 1987), including the potential consequences of anticipated increases in human presence and disturbance (Lindberg et al. 1998).

At a global scale, intertidal communities have been impacted by human activities (Liddle 1975, Kingsford et al. 1991, Povey and Keough 1991, Keough et al. 1993, Menge and Branch 2001) and one of the primary capabilities and intents of the SWAN Nearshore monitoring program is to provide early detection of change in nearshore communities and to separate human from natural causes of change. Because of the critical nature of intertidal habitats for both breeding and foraging, black oystercatchers are particularly sensitive indicators to disturbances in the nearshore (Lindberg et al. 1998). Recognized sources of disturbance include oil spills (Andres 1997, 1999, Irons et al. 2000, Weins et al 2004), geological processes, (Lentfer and Maier 1995, Gill et al. 2004), and human influences, including domestic animals and human presence (Ainley and Lewis 1974, Andres and Falxa 1995, Lindberg et al. 1998). Specifically, black oystercatchers nest exclusively just above and adjacent to the intertidal, where eggs are laid in exposed nests consisting of depressions in pebbles, sand, gravel, and shell materials. During the 26-32 day incubation phase of reproduction, eggs are susceptible to predation by other birds (primarily corvids; Lentfer and Meier 1995) and mammals (Vermeer et al. 1992), as well as human disturbance (Stillman and Goss-Custard 2002). Similar disturbance effects occur during the flightless fledging stage, which lasts approximately 38 d (Andres and Falxa 1995). Thus, for about two months during May-August, typically when human presence in nearshore habitats is highest, black oystercatchers are actively incubating or caring for young in a habitat that affords little protection from human induced disturbances. Chronic disturbance from human activities poses a significant threat to breeding black oystercatchers, either preventing nesting activity resulting in nest abandonment (Andres 1998), or through direct mortality of eggs or chicks. Monitoring of black oystercatchers will provide a potentially powerful tool in identifying the magnitude and causes of inevitable change in Gulf of Alaska nearshore habitats and communities, particularly in response to the anticipated increased use and influence of those habitats by humans.

Inclusion of black oystercatchers into the nearshore SWAN program meets the objective of the SWAN Inventory and Monitoring program in important ways. The oystercatcher provides a portal into the ecosystem that it is exclusively dependent on for all life dependent processes. Because the species is sensitive to human disturbance, nest occupancy provides an effective metric to evaluate likely human effects. And finally because of the well documented effects of oystercatcher predation, monitoring their diet provides an ecological context for interpreting variation and change in the nearshore community.

1.3 Measurable Objective
Monitoring black oystercatchers in KATM and KEFJ is designed to answer the questions:

- How are the relative density (pairs per linear kilometer of shoreline) of black oystercatcher nests and the nest site productivity (number of chicks or eggs per nest) changing annually?

- How is the composition of prey provisioned to black oystercatcher chicks changing over time?
- How do inter-annual changes in density of black oystercatchers and composition of prey provisioned to chicks differ among locations?

2 Sampling Design

2.1 Rationale for Selecting this Sampling Design over Others

A stratified random sampling design, nested within the intensive sampling sites within each Park (also referred to as blocks; see SWAN Marine Nearshore Ecosystem Monitoring Protocol Narrative, Dean and Bodkin 2011) will be used to evaluate black oystercatcher nest density/occupancy and their diet, and to examine differences in those metrics between Parks, years, and the interaction between Parks and years. Metrics to be analyzed include nest density, nest abandonment/establishment rates, and the species composition and size distribution of prey returned to provision chicks. There are three components to data collection procedures related to black oystercatchers. Two are described in detail in this SOP; one describes methods to estimate density of nest sites and occupancy of historic nest sites and establishment of new nests. The other describes methods to obtain estimates of the species composition and size distributions of prey returned to provision chicks. The third component describes methods to estimate the abundance of black oystercatchers and is described in detail in the marine bird and mammal survey SOP.

Collection of black oystercatcher nest density/occupancy and diet data will be collected annually in two of the SWAN parks, KATM and KEFJ. Within each Park, nest density/occupancy data collection will occur along five 20 km transects centered on each intensive intertidal invertebrate and algal site within each Park (example KATM Figure. 2.1). Identification of all nests within each transect will allow estimation of nest density and visits to all nest sites in subsequent years will allow estimation of nest abandonment and establishment rates. During the visit to each nest site, shell remains of prey captured and transported to the nest site to provision chicks will be collected. From each nest site we will annually estimate the species composition and size distributions of prey brought to the nest to provision chicks. This design will allow contrasts of black oystercatcher nest density, nest occupancy rates, and size and species composition of prey among sites within a Park, among Parks, and among years. Because we have little historical data on the metrics we will be estimating, following 5 years of data collection appropriate power analyses will be conducted to inform potential revision to sampling intensity and frequency.

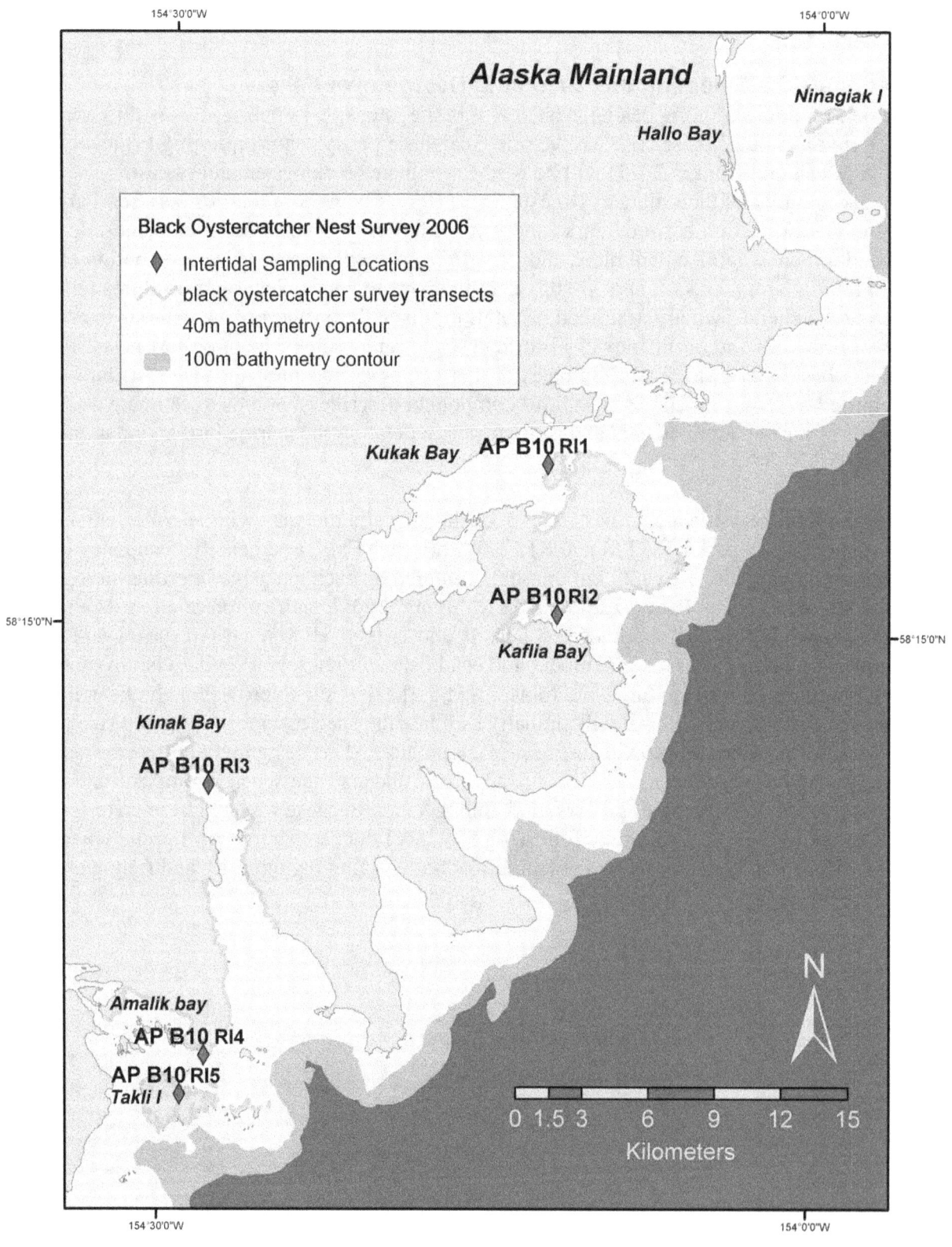

Figure 2.1. The five black oystercatcher transects, centered around rocky intertidal sampling sites in Katmai National Park (KATM). AP represents the Alaska Peninsula region and B10 represents block 10 (Katmai National Park, see Dean and Bodkin 2011).

2.2 Choosing Sampling Units

Collection of black oystercatcher nest density, nest occupancy and diet data will occur within 20 km transects centered on each of the five randomly selected intensive intertidal invertebrate and algal sampling sites within each Park. Based on an approximate nest density in Prince William Sound of about 0.1 to 0.3 nests per km (Meyers 2002) we anticipate that each transect will yield approximately 2-6 nests. The five intensive sites would yield about 10-30 nests per block. If this sampling design does not yield adequate nest sample sizes, additional transects may be added in conjunction with the marine bird and mammal surveys (see SWAN Nearshore marine bird and mammal SOP).

2.3 Recommended Frequency and Timing of Sampling

Sampling of black oystercatcher nest density, occupancy, and diet will occur annually at each intensive site within each intensive block within each park. The sampling unit will be the transect, with five transects per Park.

2.4 Level of Change that can be Detected

Because we have no historical data on the metrics of interest, we will conduct power analyses following five years of data collection to inform potential revision to sampling intensity and frequency.

3 Field Season

3.1 Observation conditions

Detection of black oystercatchers may be compromised under adverse viewing conditions, such as heavy precipitation, fog, or high winds. High sea conditions may preclude, or make landing on shorelines hazardous. In general, winds should be < 20 knots, rain absent or light, and fog should be absent. Sea conditions must allow for at least one observer to access all potential nest sites. Collections of prey shell remains should be conducted when the tide is below mean high water (MHW) to assure that prey remains below the nest are available for collection. Prey remains can be collected under most environmental conditions.

3.2 General methods- Nest density and occupancy

Transects to locate and map black oystercatcher nests should be sampled by two observers traveling slowly and methodically in small skiffs suitable for landing on rocky shorelines. Transect surveys can begin at either end of the transect and proceed to the other end, or at the center of the transect and extend to the endpoints as if there were two transects. Transects should be surveyed at speeds of approximately 5-10 knots, should parallel the shoreline as close as possible and extend to offshore islands and rock outcrops. Preferred nesting habitat includes gently sloping, treeless, small islets and rocky outcrops that at least remain partially exposed during spring tides (Andres 1998), and preferred foraging habitat includes gently sloping shorelines and mussel beds. Observers should search the shorelines and intertidal zone for black oystercatchers with the aid of high resolution binoculars. Upon detection of one or more black oystercatchers the observers should monitor the behavior of the birds to aid in identifying nest sites. Potential nest sites should be searched on foot taking care not to damage eggs or chicks (Figures 3.1-3.3). Nests, eggs, and chicks are cryptic and caution must be exercised. Nests and chicks can be difficult to detect, and the determination of an active nest site can be determined by the behavior of the adults (e.g. feinting injury, Figure 3.4). A GPS should be employed to identify the track line of the survey skiff and identify the positions of all Oystercatcher nests.

Figure 3.1.Black oystercatcher nest site.

Figures 3.2 and 3.3. Black oystercatcher chicks near their nest sites.

Figure 3.4. Black oystercatcher parent feinting injury to lure threats away from eggs or chicks.

Observers should have detailed shoreline maps with the locations of known historic nest sites. These sites should be carefully searched with binoculars and on foot to determine the current status of the nest as either active (eggs or chicks), abandoned (known prior nest, no eggs, chicks, or adults), or failed (presence of egg shell or dead chicks, or presence of adults). Nest sites not previously detected should be noted on the maps, a new waypoint on the survey track line established, and the coordinates in latitude and longitude in decimal degrees (NAD 83) recorded.

Diet- Collection of shell remains from prey brought to nests to provision chicks provides a proven method to determine black oystercatcher diet (Webster 1941, Frank 1982, Marsh 1986, Lindberg et al. 1987). Following location of either a new or prior nest and during the search for eggs, or chicks, the observers should also be searching for the presence of shell remains indicative of adult birds provisioning their chicks (Fig. 3.5). Not all nest sites will have prey remains. For example if eggs are not hatched or are depredated prior to hatching, shell prey remains may be absent. Generally, the longer post-hatching the nest visit occurs, the greater number of prey remains should be present. It is important for this reason, as well as others related to minimizing the potential effects of phenology on data collected, that nest visits be conducted as close as possible to the same date each year. Further, in order to maximize the dietary data nest visits should be conducted after 15 June of each year and as near as possible in time to historic data. Assemblages of shell remains indicative of an active nest will generally be concentrated near the nest site (< ~10 m). Care must be taken to collect all shell remains available, regardless of size, although from the literature prey less than 10 mm in size are rarely taken. All shell remains attributable to oystercatcher foraging should be collected and placed into a zip-loc bag, with an identification tag that includes date, time, name of observer, the unique nest site number, and GPS coordinates of collection site. The bag should be labeled with the date, time, and GPS coordinates. A list of species commonly brought to nest sites to provision young and the proportions of each prey type are provided in Table 3.1.

Figure 3.5. Example of shell remains collected from a black oystercatcher nest site in KATM.

Table 3.1. Prey typically consumed by black oystercatchers, and proportions of prey type in diet (ranges of values in 4th column include effects of habitat type) (sources Webster 1941[1], Andres 1998[2], Andres and Falxa 1995[3]).

Prey type	% in diet Sitka[1]	% in diet (chicks) Prince William Sound[2]	% in diet Prince William Sound[3]
Mussels (Mytilus, Modiolus)	35	42	12-43
Limpets (Acmaea, Lottia, Tectura	44	48	6-82
Chitons (Katharina)	5	3	2-48
Clams	-	6	0-60
Other (whelks, other snails)	1	-	-

3.3 Field Season Preparation

In preparation of data collection the following equipment and supplies should be compiled and tested for operation:

Skiff: The skiff and engines used to conduct surveys and access shorelines should be serviced and tested for operation. Equipment to carry on board include; an anchor, with chain and line, paddles or oars, a bilge pump or bailing device, spare parts for vessel and engine (e.g. valves, patch kit, spare prop, tools), fuel container and fuel line, epirb, and vhf radio.

Binoculars: One pair per observer, high resolution 10X.

GPS: One per each observer set to display and record data in NAD 83 datum and capable of determining a position. The GPS must be capable of recording a trackline and storing user defined waypoints (coordinates, in decimal degrees) that correspond to each nest site. GPS should have compass capability and should be used in degrees magnetic.

Data sheets: A minimum of 2 datasheets (double sided) per day should be available. Data sheets should be printed on plastic or other waterproof paper (see Tables 3.2 and 3.3).

Maps: A set of maps of each transect with shorelines, intensive intertidal invertebrate and algal sites, and known nest sites identified should be made.

Data codes: Each observer should have a copy of the data dictionary printed on plastic paper and bound to the clipboard.

Data entry procedure and electronic data file for data entry. Data will be entered into a digital spreadsheet that is structured similarly to Tables 3.2.

Miscellaneous supplies: Each observer should have a clipboard and 2 pencils, maps of transects and known nest sites, optical drying and cleaning supplies and appropriate safety equipment. Each observer should have a radio or other communication device to coordinate data collection activities among observers.

Field personnel must be dressed appropriately for extended periods outdoors in wet and windy weather. Rain pants, jacket, and boots are recommended. Spare dry socks, gloves and a hat should be carried.

Safety equipment: Each observer should carry at a minimum the following safety equipment; a hand held radio with spare batteries, food and water for 3 days, a signaling device (e.g. mirror, flares), a flashlight, and a fire starting kit.

3.4 Sequence of Events During Field Season

Black oystercatcher surveys of nest density and occupancy will be conducted annually along a 20 km transect centered at each of the five intensive intertidal invertebrate and algal sampling sites. Transects will be sampled from a small skiff suitable for accessing coastlines. Personnel may be supported by a larger vessel that provides lodging and meals. Each transect will be sampled in one or two days and all new and previous nest sites will be examined to determine current nest status as either active (eggs or chicks), abandoned (no eggs, chicks, or adults), or failed (presence of adults, but no evidence of viable reproduction e.g. chicks or prey remains, but may include egg fragments or dead chicks). Following determination of nest status, prey remains, if present, will be collected. Care must be taken throughout all nest site visits to minimize disturbance to adults, eggs, and chicks, specifically avoiding crushing of eggs or chicks.

3.5 Recording Data

3.5.1 Nest Density and Occupancy

Each nest density/occupancy transect will be uniquely identified by the SWAN Park (AP refers to the Alaska Peninsula (Katmai NP) or KP (Kenai Peninsula, Kenai Fjords NP), block number (block 10 for Katmai and block 5 for Kenai Fjords NP's) and unique number corresponding to the intertidal invertebrate and algal intensive sampling location (Fig. 2.1). Each new and previously occupied nest site will be numbered sequentially from 01 for each transect. Each nest site numbered will retain that number for the duration of the study, and be uniquely identified by the region/block/intensive site/nest number/year nest was first documented (e.g. KP_B5_RI1_1-KP refers to the Kenai Peninsula Region, Kenai Fjords National Park (B5), Rocky Intertidal site #1 (RI1) and the first nest located in 2008 (1-08)) and the associated GPS coordinates. Transect survey data will include the survey vessel track line recorded in the GPS, and a waypoint with the unique identifier number as defined above. Associated with each new or previous nest site will be the status of the nest site in the current year as either active (eggs or chicks and one or more adults present), abandoned (no eggs, chicks, or adults present), or failed (presence of adults, but no evidence of reproduction e.g. chicks or prey remains). The track line and nest waypoints will be recorded in the GPS and on a data sheet (Table 3.1, and 3.2 if prey remains are collected). Nest naming procedures are critical, if unsure of the procedure seek assistance.

Table 3.2. Data collection form for black oystercatcher nest density/occupancy and diet data.

Park		Intensive site #	Date	Survey time start	Survey time end
Observers		Cloud cover (%)	Wind (knots)	Precipitation Y/N	Visibility (km)

Nest site #	Coordinates (NAD 83)	Status (A/AB/F)	# Adults	# Eggs	# Chicks	Prey collected (Y/N)

3.5.2 Diet

Black oystercatcher diet will be determined through collection of prey shell remains when they are present, from each nest site. Prey shell remains can be identified by their clumped distribution near the nest site where adults bring prey to provision their chicks, and by their preference for mussels and limpets, and occasionally clams, chitons and snails (Table 3.1 and Fig. 3.5). Collections of shell prey remains must be systematic and inclusive of all species and sizes. Shells should be placed in a zip-loc bag with a tag placed in the bag that includes date, time, name of observer, the unique nest site number, and GPS coordinates in latitude/longitude in decimal degrees of the collection site. The bag should also be labeled with the same date, time, nest site # and GPS coordinates.

15

3.6 Post-collection Processing of Data

3.6.1 Diet

Collections of shell prey remains should be processed within 2 days. Processing includes, sorting, identification and enumeration of each item by species. For each shell the total length of the specimen will be measured with vernier calipers to the nearest mm, and entered into an electronic data base (Table 3.3). Mussel lengths are the maximum length along the longitudinal axis, limpet and clam size is the maximum diameter in mm, and chiton size is the maximum length mm. The chiton, *Katharina tunicate,* may be desiccated and difficult to measure. To the extent possible the measurement should reflect the length of the animal flattened dorso-ventrally. Consumed chitons may be represented by shell fragments that may not be measurable, but should be included in the species composition with no size assigned. Unidentified chitons should be identified as such. Other prey shell remain should be collected and measured, if possible, as appropriate to the species (e.g. urchins as maximum test diameter in mm). Following identification and measuring, prey shell remains can be discarded. Specimens that cannot be identified should be retained and preserved appropriately for future identification.

After each field day, the following tasks are to be completed:

- Field personnel are to review data sheets and edit as necessary to improve legibility and resolve any discrepancies.
- Make identifications (if possible) of any taxa for which field identifications were in question and revise taxa names on data sheets accordingly.
- Enter data from data sheets into computer files. Verify the data entry.
- Make a backup copy (cd or other removable media) of all data collected.
- Check and replace batteries in electronic equipment as needed.
- Provide a summary of activities and observations for the day including any problems, suggestions for modifications in procedures, and unusual occurrences or observations.
- Prepare field sheets and equipment for the following day's use.

After each field trip or cruise, the following are to be completed:
- Produce a summary of the cruise or field trip based on summaries of daily activities and observations

Table 3.3 Data entry format for black oystercatcher diet data.

Nest site #	Date	Species	Length (mm)

3.7 End-of-season Procedures

At the end of each field season all equipment should be cleaned and serviced as necessary and batteries removed for storage. Optics, tripods, and other equipment should be assessed for repair or replacement needs. Skiffs and engines should be winterized and prepared for seasonal storage. After each field season, the following are to be done:
- Clean and check all mechanical, optical, and electronic equipment and field gear for needed repair and store appropriately.
- Make repairs or obtain replacements for damaged or lost equipment.
- Replace disposable supplies (e.g. zip-loc bags).
- Produce a field season summary report based on daily and cruise reports.

4 Data Handling, Analysis and Reporting

4.1 Metadata Procedures

The black oystercatcher nest density/occupancy and diet data collection procedure is designed to meet two objectives. One is to estimate the density and occupancy rate (abandoned/establishment) of nest sites and the other is to estimate the species composition and mean sizes of invertebrate prey recovered by foraging adult oystercatchers. These data will be used to evaluate change over time in these attributes within the two SWAN parks, KATM and KEFJ. These data will be used to evaluate changes in nest density/occupancy rates over time and to evaluate changes in black oystercatcher diet over time.

The data collection form, data dictionary and anticipated prey species are provided in Appendix A.

4.2 Overview of Database Design

Currently, data is stored in GIS files and flat files. A database will be developed, most likely in cooperation with the US Forrest Service due to similar survey approaches, once several years of data are collected and best methods for entry, checking, storing, analyzing and reporting are finalized.

4.3 Data Entry, Verification and Editing

Data currently is entered from field datasheets into Microsoft Excel. Data is entered as soon as possible upon returning from the field. Raw data files are backed-up and the project manager verifies that data within the Excel spreadsheets matches the hardcopy recorded by the observer. The project manager edits data to correct discrepancies.

4.4 Routine Data Summaries and Statistical Analyses

The overall analytical approach is described in the SWAN Marine Nearshore Ecosystem Monitoring Protocol (Dean and Bodkin 2011 draft) that relies on data collected from most sampling protocols. In preparation of providing data derived from this data collection, annual summaries should be completed.

Annual data analysis will include summary statistics of the following:

4.4.1 Nest density, nest abandonment, nest establishment, and nest failure rates

- Total number, mean, and standard error (se) of active, abandoned, new, and failed nest sites, per transect and per Park.
- Nest abandonment rate, calculated as the number nests that are abandoned in year, i+1, divided by active nests in year i. For example in year i there were 10 active nests in transect AP-B10-RI3, and in the following year (i+1), 1 of those nests was abandoned. The resulting abandonment rate = 1/10 = 0.10. This rate should be calculated for each transect and for all transects within a Park.
- Conversely, a new nest establishment rate should be calculated as the sum of prior and new nest sites in year i+1, divided by the sum of active prior and new nest sites in year i, e.g. 12 total nests in year i+1 divided by the total of 10 active nest sites in year i. The resulting nest establishment rate = 12/10 = 1.2.

- Failed nest rates will be calculated by dividing the number of nests classified as failed by the number of active nests, e.g. 3 nests were classified as failed and 10 as active, the nest failure rate = 3 divided by 10 = 0.30. Note: while the transect may be an appropriate sample unit for calculating nest density, nest abandonment, establishment, and failure rates, may be more appropriately calculated at the block (Park) level, depending on the number of nests abandoned, established, or failed in a year.
- The average number of eggs and chicks per nest will be calculated on a per transect basis and the mean of the five transects will be used to estimate averages for each Park.

4.4.2 Diet
The following will be calculated by nest, by transect, and by Park.
- For each nest site where prey is collected, a list of species and the total number of each species will be calculated.
- For each nest site where prey are collected, frequency of occurrence will be calculated by dividing the total number of specimens collected by the number of each species (e.g. 60 shell remains total were collected of which 30 were mussels (*Mytilus trossolus*) the frequency of occurrence of mussels is 30/60 = 0.50. Following calculating frequency of occurrence by species, taxonomically similar species may be grouped (e.g. *Mytilus* and *Modiolus* grouped as mussels).
- Mean sizes (se) will be calculated for each species and for each taxonomic group where appropriate.
- Size class distributions will be generated for all common species, by nest. A pooled size class distribution by transect and Park will be generated by randomly selecting 10 individuals of a species for each nest within the block that contains 10 or more individuals.

Analysis of annual data over time will include the following:

Nest density, nest abandonment, nest establishment, and nest failure rates
- Multivariate analysis of variance (manova) will be used to make between Park comparisons of nest density, nest abandonment, nest establishment, and nest failure rates over time.
- Trends in the variables estimated (nest density, nest abandonment, nest establishment, and nest failure rates) will be plotted over time. As time series of data increases, multiple regression procedures will be used to evaluate relations between nest density and nest abandonment, nest establishment, and nest failure rates, by Park.

Diet
- Chi-square analysis will be used to compare the frequency of occurrence and size class distributions of common prey species among nests within transects, among transects within Parks and among Parks.
- Analysis of variance (anova) will be used to compare mean sizes of common prey species among nests within transects and among transects within Parks. - Trends in the variables estimated (frequency of occurrence of a species and mean prey sizes) will be plotted over time. As time series of data increases, multiple regression procedures will be used to evaluate relations between prey frequency and mean prey size and nest density, nest abandonment, nest establishment, and nest failure rates, by Park.

4.5 Report Format

Reports will conform to specific guidelines set by the Natural Resource Publications Management website (http://www.nature.nps.gov/publications/NRPM/index.cfm). Reports will include maps, graphs, figures and other visuals to facilitate comprehension of findings.

4.6 Methods for Trend Analyses

Refer to the SWAN Protocol Narrative for Marine Nearshore Ecosystem Monitoring (Dean and Bodkin 2011 Draft).

4.7 Data Archival Procedures

Refer to the SWAN Protocol Narrative for Marine Nearshore Ecosystem Monitoring (Dean and Bodkin 2011 Draft).

4.8 Reporting

Refer to the SWAN Protocol Narrative for Marine Nearshore Ecosystem Monitoring (Dean and Bodkin 2011 Draft).

5 Personnel Requirements and Training

5.1 Roles and Responsibilities
A minimum of two observers are required to complete this SOPS and each observer must be capable of identifying black oystercatchers with the aid of high resolution binoculars. The observers must be familiar with the habits and habitats of the species and identifying characteristics of its most common prey, mussels, and limpets. The observers must be able to identify oystercatcher behavior indicative of nest/chick protection, and in recognizing nests with and without eggs, and oystercatcher chicks. The observers must be capable and willing to work in small skiffs and should have the physical ability to access rocky shoreline in adverse sea conditions to perform assigned duties. Only observers with experience surveying black oystercatchers and visiting at least 10 nest sites should hold primary data collection responsibility.

At least one of the pair of observers must be trained and experienced in the operation of small vessels in open sea conditions and in accessing rocky shorelines with a small skiff. Observer training should consist of assisting an experienced observer for at least 10 nest visits and 100 km of nest survey experience. Based on simultaneous observations, an experienced observer may grant primary observer status to a trainee, based on the ability of the trainee to quickly and accurately identify Oystercatchers, their nest, eggs, and chicks, and their prey.

6 Operational Requirements and Workloads

6.1 Operational Requirements
Operational requirements include transportation and access to each of the intensive intertidal invertebrate and algal sampling sites within each Park, access and use of required optics and electronics (e.g. GPS), and access to taxonomic keys and guides to marine invertebrates common to the Gulf of Alaska.

6.2 Annual Workload and Field Schedule
Workload requires 10 person days per year for field data collection (1 person day per site x's 5 sites x's 2 Parks), and 20 person days for lab and data analysis and reporting. Access to sites and observation locations attained through small skiffs.

6.3 Facility and Equipment Needs
Equipment requirements to successfully conduct black oystercatcher surveys include a small skiff (holds 3-4 people), sufficient staff to observe and assist in field procedures, marine safety equipment (hand held radios, flares), binoculars and GPS units for electronic data recording during flights, home base computers (for data management, pre-season transect selection and mapping, and data analysis), a printer and plotter, and hand fuel pumps with associated fueling equipment.

6.4 Start-up Costs and Budget Considerations
Startup costs include $1,000 for 2 GPS units and $500 for miscellaneous field supplies such as field guides, clipboards, paper, zip-loc bags, calipers, etc. Annual operating budget estimated at

approximately $15,000 for 2 Parks, consisting of 10 d of vessel charter @$1,200/d, plus fuel and food. However, vessel charter costs that will be required to support this protocol are included under the sea otter foraging data collection protocol. Therefore annual field costs of implementing this protocol must be considered dependent on the sea otter foraging protocol. Annual costs of data management, manipulation, analysis and reporting are estimated at 20 days.

7 Procedures for Revising the Protocol

All edits and amendments made to the protocol narrative and/or SOPs should be recorded in the revision history log table at the beginning of this document. Users of this protocol should promptly notify the project leader of the nearshore marine monitoring program of recommended edits or changes. The project leader will review and incorporate suggested changes as necessary, record these changes in the revision history log, and modify the date and version number on the title page of this document to reflect these changes.

It is anticipated that following at least five years of annual data collection it will be important to evaluate, in terms of power and sensitivity, the ability of the sampling design to detect change in the data derived from black oystercatcher data collection protocols. Following such analyses it may be appropriate to consider revising sampling design or data collection protocols.

8 Literature Cited

Ainley, D. G. and T. J. Lewis. 1974. The history of Farallon Island marine bird populations, 1854-1972. The Condor 76:432-446.

Andres, B. A., and G. A. Falxa. 1995. Black Oystercatcher (*Haematopus bachmani*). *In* The Birds of North America, No. 155 (A. Poole and F. Gill, eds.).The Academy of Natural Sciences, Philadelphia, and The American Ornithologists' Union, Washington, D.C.

Andres, B. A. 1997. The *Exxon Valdez* oil spill disrupted the breeding of Black Oystercatchers. J. of Wild. Manage. 61:1322-1328.

Andres, B. A. 1998. Shoreline habitat use of Black Oystercatchers breeding in Prince William Sound, Alaska. Journal of Field Ornithology 69:626-634.

Andres, B. A. 1998. Black Oystercatcher *Haematopus bachmani*. Restoration Notebook, Exxon Valdez Oil Spill Trustee Council, Anchorage AK 8pp.

Andres, B. A. 1999. Effects of persistent shoreline oil on breeding success and chick growth in Black Oystercatcher. The Auk 116:640-650. Brown, S., C. Hickey, B. Harrington, and R. Gill. 2001. The U.S. Shorebird Conservation Plan, 2nd ed. Manomet Center for Conservation Sciences, Manomet, MA. Brown, S., Hickey, C., Harrington, B., and Gill, R. eds.

Chugach National Forest. Forest Plan Monitoring and Evaluation Report Fiscal Year 2003. 2003.

Dean, T. and J. Bodkin. 2011. Draft Final Protocol Narrative for Marine Nearshore Ecosystem Monitoring, Southwest Alaska Network. Report to the National Park Service. Anchorage, AK. 57 pp.

Falxa, G.A. 1992. Prey choice and habitat use by foraging Black Oystercatchers; interactions between prey quality, habitat availability, and age of bird. Ph.D. dissertation, University of California, Davis.Frank, P. W. 1982. Effects of Winter Feeding on Limpets byblack oystercatchers, *Haematopus bachmani*. Ecology 63:1352-1362.

Groves, S. 1982. Aspects of foraging in Black Oystercatchers (Aves: Haematopodidae). PhD dissertation. University of British Columbia, Vancouver, BC.

Gill, V. A., S. A. Hatch, and R. B. Lanctot. 2004. Colonization, population growth, and nesting success of Black Oystercatchers following a seismic uplift. The Condor 106:791-800. Groves, S. 1984. Chick growth, sibling rivalry, and chick production in Americanblack oystercatchers. The Auk 101:525-531.

Hahn, T. and M. Denny. 1989. Tenacity-mediated selective predation by oystercatchers on intertidal limpets and its role in maintaining habitat partitioning by "Collisella"scabra and Lottia digitalis. Marine ecology progress series. Oldendorf 53:1-10.

Hazlitt, S. and R. W. Butler. 2001. Site fidelity and reproductive success of Black Oystercatchers in British Columbia. Waterbirds 24:203-207.

Irons, D. B., S. J. Kendall, W. P. Erickson, L. L. McDonald, and B. K. Lance. 2000. Nine Years After the Exxon Valdez Oil Spill: Effects on Marine Bird Populations in Prince William Sound, Alaska. The Condor 102:723-737.

Keough, M. J., G. P. Quinn, and A. King. 1993. Correlations between human collection and intertidal mollusk populations on rocky shores. Conservation Biology 7:378-390.

Kingsford, M. J., A. J. Underwood, and S. J. Kennelly. 1991. Humans as predators on rocky reefs in New South Wales, Australia. Marine Ecology Progress Series. Oldenforf 72:1-14.

Knox, G. A. 2000. The Ecology of Seashores. CRC Press LLC.

Lentfer, H. P. and A. J. Maier. Breeding ecology of the Black Oystercatcher in the Beardslee Island region of Glacier Bay National Park. Proceedings of the Third Glacier Bay Science Symposium. 1995.

Liddle, M. J. 1975. A selective review of the ecological effects of human trampling on natural ecosystems. Biological Conservation 7:17-36.

Lindberg, D. R., K. I. Warheit, and J. A. Estes. 1987. Prey Preference and Seasonal Predation by Oystercatchers on Limpets at San Nicolas Island, California USA. Marine Ecology. 39.:105-113.

Lindberg, D., J. Estes, and K. Warheit. 1998. Human influences on trophic cascades along rocky shores . Ecological Applications 8:880-890.

Marsh, C. P. 1986. The Impact of Avian Predators on high intertidal limpet populations . J. Exp. Mar. Biol. Ecol. 104.:185-201.

Meyers, P. 2002. Black oystercatcher surveys of Prince William Sound: 2002 final report. Unpublished report by U.S. Forest Service, Chugach National Forest, Cordova Ranger District.

Meese, R. J. Effects of Predation by Birds on Rocky Intertidal Community Structure. Bull. Ecol. Soc. Am. 71 [2], 250. 1990.

Menge, B. A. and G. M. Branch. Rocky intertidal communities. 2001. Bertness, Mark D. Gaines Steve D. Hay Mark E. Marine Community Ecology. 221-251. Sunderland, Massachusetts, Sinauer Associates, Inc.

Meyers, P. 2002. Black oystercatcher surveys of Prince William Sound: 2002 final report. Unpublished report by U.S. Forest Service, Chugach National Forest, Cordova Ranger

District.Povey, A. and M. J. Keough. 1991. Effects of trampling on plant and animal populations on rocky shores. Oikos 61:355-368.

Power, M. E., D. Tilman, J. A. Estes, B. A. Menge, W. J. Bond, L. S. Mills, G. Daily, J. C. Castilla, J. Lubchenco, and R. T. Paine. 1996. Challenges in the quest for keystones. BioScience 46:609-620.

Stillman, R. A. and J. D. Goss-Custard. 2002. Seasonal changes in the response of Oystercatchers *Haematopus ostralegus* to human disturbance. Journal of Avian Biology 33:358-365.

Vermeer, K., K. H. Morgan, and G. E. J. Smith. 1992. black oystercatcher habitat selection, reproductive success, and their relationship with Glaucous-winged gulls. Colonial Waterbirds 15:14-23.

Webster, J. D. 1941. Feeding habitats of the Black Oyster-catcher. The Condor 43:175-180.

Weins, J. A., R. H. Day, S. M. Murphy, and K. R. Parker. 2004. Changing habitat and habitat use by birds after the *Exxon Valdez* oil spill, 1989-2001. Ecological Applications 14:1806-1825.

Wootton, J. T. 1992. Indirect Effects, Prey Susceptibility, and Habitat Selection: Impacts of Birds on Limpets and Algae. Ecology 73:981-991.

Appendix A: Data Dictionaries

Data dictionary for data fields in Table 3.2.

Header data

Park: The SWAN Park in which the data were collected: **KP** (Kenai Peninsula, KEFJ) or **AP** (Alaska Peninsula, KATM)

Intensive site #: The number (**e.g. RI13**) of the intensive intertidal invertebrate and algal sampling site associated with this data collection.

Date: Day month year, with day and year in numerals and month in letters (e.g. 14 June 2007

Survey start and survey end time: Use the 24 hour clock (e.g. **0745**).

Observers: First and last names of observers (e.g. **Bill Smith**).

Cloud cover: Percent of sky obscured by cloud cover, estimated in 10% increments (e.g. **30%**).

Wind: Velocity of wind estimated in knots (e.g. **10** knots).

Precipitation: Is it raining at the start survey time (e.g. **Y**=yes or **N**=no).

Visibility: What is the estimated horizontal visibility at the survey start time, at sea level, in km, and tenths of km at values < **1.0** km).

Tabular data

Nest site #: The alpha numeric code uniquely identified by the SWAN Park (**KP or AP**) and unique number corresponding to the intertidal invertebrate and algal intensive sampling location within that intensive block (e.g. **KP_RI3_0711**, represents the Kenai Fjords Park, intensive intertidal invertebrate and algal site number 3, and black oystercatcher nest number 11 in 2007).

Coordinates (LATITUDE LONGITUDE IN DECIMAL DEGREES, NAD 83): The latitude and longitude in decimal degrees in NAD 83, at the nest site #.

Status: The status of the oystercatcher nest site; **A**= Active nest, adults, and evidence of eggs or chicks (e.g. defensive adult behavior), **AB**= Abandoned nest, no evidence of adults, eggs, or chicks, and **F**= Failed nest, adults present but no evidence of eggs, or chicks (e.g. no defensive adult behavior).

 # Adults: Number of adult oystercatchers observed in association with nest (e.g. **1** or **2**).

 # Eggs: Number of eggs in or associated with nest, **0** if none, if present usually **1-3**, occasionally **4**.

 # Chicks: Number of chicks detected at nest site, **0-3**, occasionally **4**).

Prey collected: Were oystercatcher shell prey remain collected (**Y/N**)

Data dictionary for data fields in Table 3.3, Black oystercatcher diet.

Header data

Park: The SWAN Park in which the data were collected: **KP** (Kenai Peninsula, KEFJ) or **AP** (Alaska Peninsula, KATM)

Intensive site #: The number (**RI1-5**) of the intensive intertidal invertebrate and algal sampling site associated with this data collection.

Coordinates LATITUDE LONGITUDE IN DECIMAL DEGREES, NAD 83): The latitude and longitude in decimal degrees in NAD 83, at the nest site #.

Date: Day month year, with day and year in numerals and month in letters (e.g. 14 June 2007

Start time of collection: Use the 24 hour clock (e.g. **0745**).

Observers: First and last names of observers (e.g. **Bill Smith**).

Tabular data

Nest site #: The alpha numeric code uniquely identified by the SWAN Park (**KP or AP**) and unique number corresponding to the intertidal invertebrate and algal intensive sampling location within that intensive block (e.g. **KP_RI3_0711**, represents the Kenai Fjords Park, intensive intertidal invertebrate and algal site number 3, and black oystercatcher nest number 11 in 2007).

Species: Genus and species of shell remain collected.

List of species likely to be encountered, others should be added as genus and species.

Mussels

Mytilus trossolus
Mytilus californians
Modiolus modiolus
Musculus niger
Musculus musculus

Snails

Littorina spp
Nucella spp.

Limpets

Acmaea spp.
Lottia digitalis
Lottia pelta
Lottia strigilata
Tectura persona
Tectura scutum

Chitons

Katharina tunicate
Mopalia spp.
Tonicella spp.

Barnacle

Mitella polymerus
Balanus spp.
Semibalanus spp.
Chthamalus spp.

Worms

Nereis spp.

Clams

Protothaca staminea
Saxidomus giganteus
Clinocardium nuttallii

Crabs

of unidentified species and urchins (*Strongylocentrotus* spp) may also be encountered.

Length: Total length in mm. For each shell the total length of the specimen will be measured with vernier calipers to the nearest mm, and entered into an electronic data base (Table 3). Mussel lengths are the maximum length along the longitudinal axis, limpet and clam size is the maximum diameter in mm, and chiton size is the maximum length mm. Consumed chitons may be represented by shell fragments that may not be measurable, but should be included in the species composition with no size assigned. Unidentified chitons should be identified as such. Other prey shell remain should be collected and measured, if possible, as appropriate to the species (e.g. urchins as maximum test diameter in mm). The chiton, *Katharina tunicate*, may be desiccated and difficult to measure. To the extent possible the measurement should reflect the length of the animal flattened dorso-ventrally.

NPS 953/107685, May 2011